OUR ANGRY PLANET

Volcanoes

ANNE ROONEY

Adapted from an original text by Anita Ganeri

W
FRANKLIN WATTS
LONDON • SYDNEY

First published in 2009 by Franklin Watts

Franklin Watts
338 Euston Road
London NW1 3BH

Franklin Watts Australia
Level 17/207 Kent Street, Sydney, NSW 2000

Produced by Arcturus Publishing Limited,
26/27 Bickels Yard, 151–153 Bermondsey Street, London SE1 3HA

Our Angry Planet is based on the series *Nature's Fury*, published by Franklin Watts.

Editor: Alex Woolf
Designer: Mind's Eye Design and Mike Reynolds

Picture Credits
Corbis: 23 (Roger Ressmeyer), 27 (Reuters).
Frank Lane Picture Agency: 10.
NASA: 18 (Jeff Schmaltz, MODIS Rapid Response Team, NASA/GSFC), 20 (Landsat 7 project and EROS Data Center), 21 (Jacques Descloitres, MODIS Rapid Response Team, NASA/GSFC).
Rex Features: 9 (The Travel Library), 12 (Sipa Press), 13 (Sipa Press), 14 (Rich/Wasaki), 22 (Eye Ubiquitous), 25 (Mauro Carraro), 26 (Mauro Carraro).
Science Photo Library: 4 (Krafft/Explorer), 5 (G. Brad Lewis), 6 (Simon Fraser), 7 (Gary Hincks), 8 (Gary Hincks), 11 (Ray Fairbanks), 15 (Bernhard Edmaier), 16 (Dennis Flaherty), 17 (Tony Craddock), 19 (Stephen and Donna O'Meara), 24 (Krafft/Hoa-Qui), 28 (Adam G. Sylvester), 29 (Anne Kahle, JPL-Caltech).
Shutterstock: cover (juliengrondin).

Every attempt has been made to clear copyright. Should there be any inadvertent omission, please apply to the publisher for rectification.

A CIP catalogue record for this book is available from the British Library.

Dewey Decimal Classification Number: 551.21

ISBN 978 0 7496 9051 9

Printed in China

Franklin Watts is a division of Hachette Children's Books, an Hachette UK Company
www.hachette.co.uk

Contents

What are **Volcanoes?**

▼ **A fountain of lava shoots from a volcano in Indonesia.**

A volcano is a hill or mountain that spurts out hot, **molten** rock. The molten rock is called **lava**. It comes from deep underground. Volcanic eruptions are spectacular and violent. They produce red-hot rivers of lava, huge clouds of **ash** and thick flows of mud. The volcano builds up from cold, hardened lava and ash.

Volcanoes have erupted since the Earth began, 4,500 million years ago. About 25 erupt each year on land. Some eruptions are massive explosions. Others produce gentle fountains of lava. Volcanoes can erupt nearly all the time, or only every few hundred years.

Volcanoes and the landscape

Much of the Earth's surface is made of rock from volcanic eruptions. Volcanoes can build and destroy landscapes. They make new islands and mountains. However, they can also cover land with mud, ash and lava. Big eruptions burn forests, farms and homes and kill thousands of people.

Vulcan's island

The Romans believed a god called Vulcan lived inside a volcano on an island. They said he made weapons for the other gods. They thought the fire they saw coming from the island Vulcano was sparks from his **forge**.

◀ **This school bus was trapped in hot lava. When the lava cooled it went hard. The bus is stuck forever.**

CASE STUDY

Krakatau, 1883

One of the biggest eruptions in history happened in 1883. The Indonesian island of Krakatau blew apart in a massive explosion. The noise was so loud that people heard it 5,000 kilometres away. Hot **ash clouds** and giant waves swamped the area. More than 36,000 people died.

How do Volcanoes Form?

▼ Iceland is on a boundary beween tectonic plates. The rocks are being torn apart as the plates move. There are huge cracks in the land.

Volcanoes form where **molten** rock pushes up through the Earth. When it is underground, the hot rock is called **magma**. It comes from the Earth's mantle. The mantle lies under the hard surface of the Earth, the Earth's **crust**. The crust is about 50 kilometres thick on land. Under the ocean, it is only about five kilometres thick.

Moving plates

The Earth's crust is broken into large plates. These are called **tectonic plates**. They move very slowly on top of the mantle. The mantle flows slowly beneath them. The plates move only a few centimetres a year. Most volcanoes occur where two plates meet. The magma leaks up through the join.

Plates meet at **boundaries**. In some places the plates push together at boundaries. One plate is pushed under the other. The one that is pushed down melts and makes magma. The magma comes out in volcanoes. This kind of meeting place is called a **destructive boundary**. At other places the plates move apart. The gap is filled by magma coming up from beneath. This kind of meeting place is called a **constructive boundary**.

Undersea volcanoes

There are more volcanoes under the sea than on land. Most are at constructive boundaries where plates move apart. These boundaries are called **spreading ridges**. The magma goes hard, making new land each side of the boundary.

◄ Oahu in Hawaii, USA, is the tip of a hot-spot volcano. Magma leaks up from far below.

HOT-SPOT VOLCANOES

Some volcanoes grow in the middle of tectonic plates. They form over **hot spots** where magma forces its way up. The islands of Hawaii in the Pacific Ocean are the tops of huge, undersea hot-spot volcanoes.

Inside a **Volcano**

The top of a volcano has a dent, called a **crater**. Under the crater is a long tunnel. This is the **vent**. It goes down to the **magma chamber** where the **magma** collects. The magma chamber can be hundreds of kilometres down. When the volcano erupts, magma rushes up the vent and out of the volcano.

Composite cones

There are different types of volcano. Most volcanoes on land are cone-shaped. They are called **composite cones** or stratovolcanoes. They are like giant heaps of rubble, made of layers of **ash** and broken **lava** from old eruptions. They grow over thousands or millions of years. Magma leaks between the layers and goes hard, making the volcano more stable.

▲ **A composite volcano. It has layers made during earlier eruptions. The magma rises up the vent in an eruption.**

What's in magma?

Some magma is runny, like syrup. Some is thick and sticky, like tar. It is very hot – about 1,000 degrees Celsius. There is gas in magma. Deep underground, the gas stays dissolved. When the magma comes up to the surface, the gas comes out. It bursts out of the volcano with the **molten** rock. It's like shaking a bottle of fizzy drink and then opening it.

▲ Sugarloaf Mountain in Brazil is made of magma that went hard inside the vent of a volcano. The sides of the volcano have worn away.

LIVE, SLEEPING AND DEAD

Volcanoes can be active, dormant or extinct. An active volcano is still alive. It has erupted in the last few thousand years. There are about 500 active volcanoes on Earth. A dormant volcano is active, but not erupting now – it's asleep. An extinct volcano is dead – scientists think it won't erupt again. But they could be wrong!

Shields
and Cinders

▼ Runny lava blown into the air by gases makes a lava fountain.

There are different types of eruption. Gentle eruptions make rivers of red-hot **lava**. Violent eruptions make huge **ash clouds**, but little lava. Some make **ash** and lava. Different eruptions build different types of volcano.

Shield volcanoes

Gentle eruptions make **shield volcanoes**. A shield volcano looks like an upside-down plate. It has gentle slopes and is wide and low. In an eruption, blobs of runny lava blast up in a fountain. The lava runs down the sides of the volcano and goes hard. It takes thousands or millions of years to make a mountain. Shield volcanoes happen at **hot spots** and **constructive boundaries**.

Cinder cones

Sometimes, huge blobs of lava are hurled into the air. Some lava blobs have bubbles of gas in them. The blobs cool and go hard. They fall to the ground as pieces of rock called **cinders**. Cinders pile up, making **cinder cone** volcanoes.

▲ Cinder cones in Hawaii. They often form in groups.

HAWAIIAN ERUPTIONS

Eruptions that make fountains or rivers of lava are called Hawaiian eruptions. They often happen in Hawaii. Hawaii is made up of five shield volcanoes. One of them is Kilauea. It has been erupting all the time since 1983. It makes huge lava fountains.

Explosive Volcanoes

▲ An eruption on the island of Montserrat in 1997. The island was buried under ash.

The most explosive eruptions happen at **destructive boundaries**. The **magma** is thick and sticky. It blocks up the **vent** until the pressure is too great – then it blows out in a huge, dangerous explosion. The largest explosions on Earth have been made by these volcanoes.

Plinian eruptions

The magma is so thick, gas can't bubble out. Instead, the whole lot explodes into tiny pieces. These eruptions make **composite cone** volcanoes (see page 8). They are called Plinian eruptions after a Roman named Pliny who died in an eruption of Mount Vesuvius in 79 CE.

The rock shatters into pieces smaller than a grain of sand. These are carried upwards in clouds as **ash**. The column of ash and hot gas can be 50 kilometres high.

Volcanic hurricanes

A cloud of ash and rock is heavy. Sometimes the column collapses, then rushes down the volcano. This makes a volcanic hurricane of scorching gas, ash and bits of rock. It can move at 160 kilometres per hour. A volcanic hurricane is also called a **pyroclastic flow**.

▲ This pyroclastic flow on Mount Unzen in Japan killed 40 people who were photographing it in 1991.

CASE STUDY

Mount Pinatubo, 1991

Mount Pinatubo is in the Philippines. It erupted in 1991 for the first time in 400 years. First, the mountain made rumbling noises. Finally, the top 200 metres blew off the mountain. A huge **ash cloud** turned the sky black for weeks. It was one of the biggest explosions ever seen.

Mountains and Islands

Volcanoes start as a **vent** (hole) in the ground. **Ash, cinders** and **lava** build up around the vent. Eventually, they pile up into a mountain.

▼ **Mount Fuji in Japan last erupted in 1707. It is 3,776 metres tall.**

Shield volcanoes are made from lava trickling down the side. **Cinder cones** are made from piles of loose cinders. **Composite cones** are made from ash and lava. Some volcanoes stand alone. Others are part of huge mountain ranges.

Volcanic islands

Lava from undersea volcanoes piles up on the sea floor. It makes seamounts. If these get tall enough, they become new islands. Volcanic islands form in curved lines called sea arcs. Hawaii has the tallest mountain on Earth. It is a seamount 9,000 metres tall.

Most volcanic islands form at **destructive boundaries** or **hot spots**. Some grow at **spreading ridges**.

▲ This volcanic island near Iceland has **craters made by hot gas bubbling through cooling lava.**

Fiery rocks

Rock made from volcanic lava is called igneous rock. It means 'fiery rock'. There are different kinds of igneous rock. Runny lava from shield volcanoes makes hard, black rock called basalt. The seabed is made of basalt. It forms at spreading ridges. On land, layers of volcanic ash pile up. The bottom layers are squashed together making a rock called **tuff**.

CASE STUDY

A volcano grows

In February 1943 a Mexican farmer noticed small **earthquakes** on his farm. The ground felt hot. Soon, a crack opened in his field. Lava and ash poured out. An eruption happened in front of his eyes! By July the volcano was 300 metres high and the whole village was buried. The eruption finally stopped in 1952.

Volcano Destruction

Eruptions make new rock and help to build volcanoes – but they can also be very destructive. When a **composite-cone** volcano erupts, the mountain blows apart, leaving a vast hole.

Blowing its top

Composite volcanoes eventually become unstable. Thick **magma** builds up inside the volcano, but can't get out. The huge pressure inside makes the upper slopes bulge and collapse. Massive avalanches of ash and rock spread for many kilometres.

When a composite volcano erupts, the top often blows off, leaving the mountain hundreds of metres shorter. **Ash** and rock blast into the air and pour down the mountainside.

▲ The eruption of Mount St Helens in 1980 left a huge, gaping hole.

Calderas

A **caldera** is a huge **crater**. It is made when a volcano explodes. The ground falls into the empty **magma chamber**. Small calderas are a few kilometres across. Large calderas can be 50 kilometres across or even more.

Three of the biggest calderas are in Yellowstone National Park in the USA. One is 60 kilometres across. The calderas were made 500,000 years ago in eruptions that were so powerful half of North America was buried in ash. There is still hot magma under Yellowstone. It heats the water for hot springs.

◄ Crater Lake in Oregon, USA, was made when the volcano Mount Mazama erupted and collapsed 7,700 years ago. The new island shows the volcano is still active.

CASE STUDY

Mount St Helens, 1980

The top 400 metres of Mount St Helens blew off in an eruption in 1980. There were small **earthquakes**. Next, **ash clouds** poured from the crater. The top of the mountain bulged out, then collapsed and slid downwards. Magma exploded from the mountain, blowing the top to pieces.

Environmental Effects

▼ A photograph taken from space shows ash blowing away from the volcano Mount Etna in Sicily, Italy.

Eruptions affect the land around a volcano in many ways. **Lava** flows slowly, covering and burning trees and fields. After a few kilometres, it cools and hardens. **Pyroclastic flows** and **ash** can be much more dangerous and travel a lot further.

Ash layers

Violent eruptions throw out vast clouds of ash. In 1980 enough ash came from the eruption of Mount St Helens to fill 5,000 Olympic stadiums. The ash is carried by the wind and can fall hundreds of kilometres away. Plants cannot grow through the thick ash. The landscape becomes a grey desert. Pyroclastic flows are even more dangerous. Scorching gases burn the plants and trees in their path and kill animals instantly.

Global effects

Ash from a big eruption can be carried 15 kilometres into the air. It may stay there for months and can be carried all round the world. It blocks out sunlight and makes the world a little colder. Gases from volcanoes can make acid rain. This kills plants and wildlife in lakes and rivers.

▲ The side of this volcano in the Caribbean has been stripped bare by pyroclastic flows. The ash has changed the shape of the coastline, too.

CASE STUDY

Tambora, 1815

In 1815 the island volcano Tambora erupted in Indonesia. The eruption was the largest for 10,000 years. Ash spread around the world and blocked out the sun. There were months of cold, wet weather. In the USA, 1816 was called the 'year without a summer'. Crops would not grow. People rioted because they were short of food.

Mud with Flood

After an eruption, water can mix with **ash** to make thick mud that pours down the volcano. Explosive eruptions near the sea can cause huge waves.

Mud flows

The biggest volcanoes are very high. They have ice and snow at the top. In an eruption, the ice and snow melts and flows down the mountain. It mixes with ash to make a dangerous river of thick mud. The **mud flow** is called a lahar.

▶ **Mount St Helens in the USA seen from space. The grey lines are hardened mud left by mud flows.**

The mud rushes along at up to 150 kilometres an hour. It can flow for 300 kilometres, crushing everything in its path. When it stops, it sets as hard as concrete.

Mud flows also form when ash mixes with heavy rain. The rain often comes from thunderstorms that happen inside **ash clouds**.

Monster waves

An eruption under the sea can cause a huge wave called a tsunami. Out at sea the tsunami is low, but travels very fast. When it reaches the shore, it grows much taller. It crashes over the land, destroying everything and killing many people.

▲ This photograph of Iceland from space shows the ice caps as white areas. There are volcanoes under the ice. When they erupt, the heat melts the ice, making floods.

CASE STUDY

Iceland, 1996

Iceland has many volcanoes covered with ice. When they erupt, the ice above melts. In 1996 an eruption melted enough ice to fill an Olympic swimming pool every second. The water collected for days, then poured out in a huge flood. It covered the land with ash and rock. The flood carried chunks of ice the size of houses.

Living with **Volcanoes**

One in ten of all the people in the world live near volcanoes. They are at risk of their homes being destroyed in an eruption.

Cities at risk

Many cities are built where there have been volcanic eruptions before. They are in danger from future eruptions. Naples in Italy is near Vesuvius and could be hit by **pyroclastic flows**. Parts of Seattle in the USA could be swamped by **mud flows** from Mount Rainier. People did not know the risks when they built the cities. It would be too difficult to move the cities now.

▼ **A farmer working his fields under the volcano Mayon. It is a risky place to live, but the soil is good for crops.**

Volcanic soil

Some people live near volcanoes because that is the only place available. Others choose to live there because the soil is very good for growing crops. The soil near the bottom of a volcano has lots of minerals. It is good for plants. Many coffee farms and vineyards are below volcanoes. Farmers may even go back to the same land after an eruption because the soil is so good.

Rock from volcanoes is useful for building. It can be cut to make bricks. **Cinders** are good for making roads. Heat from volcanoes can be used to heat water and make electricity.

▲ These children in Japan wear hats to go to and from school. The hats protect them from rocks thrown out by the volcano Sakurajima.

FARMING ON MAYON

The Mayon volcano is in the Philippines. It erupts about once every ten years. There is little farming land available in the area, so farmers grow crops on the slopes of Mayon. It is a risky way to live – 75 farmers died in an eruption in 1993.

Human Disaster

▼ Lava destroyed many houses on the island of Heimaey near Iceland in 1973.

Eruptions can be major disasters. They destroy towns, villages, roads and farms.

Lava is not usually dangerous. It moves so slowly that people can get out of the way. But it destroys and burns buildings. When lava covers farmland, the land is ruined. It cannot be used to grow crops for many years.

Burning and burying

Pyroclastic flows are deadly. Scorching hot winds like hurricanes tear down buildings. They are so fast that people cannot escape them, even in cars.

Mud flows are just as dangerous. They knock down buildings and set hard. **Ash** looks like dust, but it is very heavy when it is wet. It makes roofs crash down.

In an eruption, roads are blocked and bridges are destroyed by lava, mud and pyroclastic flows. Telephone cables and power lines are brought down. People cannot move around or communicate with the outside world. Ash blocks engines and machinery.

Ash and aircraft

Ash damages aircraft engines, too. In 1982 the engines of a plane flying through ash from a volcano in Indonesia failed. The plane glided for thousands of metres. Although it landed safely, the experience was terrifying for the people on the plane.

▲ Mud flows in Armero, Colombia, where nine out of ten people died in 1985.

CASE STUDY

Nevado del Ruiz, 1985

The volcano Nevado del Ruiz in Colombia erupted in 1985. Melted ice mixed with ash to make a mud flow. It poured down a valley into the town of Armero. The people were asleep, and 21,000 died. Only 2,000 escaped alive. The town is still buried under the hardened mud.

Rescue and Aid

When scientists think a big eruption is coming, they tell people to leave the area near the volcano. Sometimes the warning comes too late. Sometimes people don't want to leave their homes or don't believe the scientists.

▲ Rescuers help a survivor out of a mud flow at Armero in Colombia.

To the rescue

People caught in an eruption must be rescued. They need food and somewhere to stay. Later, they need help rebuilding their homes.

Straight after an eruption, rescue workers come to help out. They look for missing people and rescue survivors. They move survivors to a safe area. They often have to use helicopters because roads are blocked. Helicopters can rescue people from floods and **mud flows**, too.

The aftermath

Clearing up after an eruption is difficult. If there is too much **lava** or mud to clear away, people have to live somewhere else. If there is just a little, it can be cleared up. People have to rebuild houses, roads, bridges and communication links.

Sometimes people are left with nothing. Aid agencies help them find shelter and food until they can have a new home.

▲ People carry their belongings over lava flows in Goma. They took shelter in special camps.

CASE STUDY

Nyiragongo, 2002

The town of Goma in the Democratic Republic of the Congo was hit by an eruption of Mount Nyiragongo in January 2002. A third of the town was destroyed. Four hundred thousand people fled to Rwanda. Aid agencies brought food, clothes and blankets. They helped people move back to Goma. They provided clean water supplies and materials to build new homes.

Volcano Science

Scientists who study volcanoes are called vulcanologists. Studying eruptions helps them understand how volcanoes work. They try to work out when an eruption will happen. Then they can tell people to move out of the way. It is a difficult job, as all eruptions are different.

▼ A vulcanologist uses a long probe to measure the temperature of lava. His shiny suit reflects heat to protect him.

Measuring layers

Vulcanologists measure the layers of **ash**, **lava**, rock and mud around volcanoes. They work out when eruptions happened in the past and how violent the eruptions were. This shows how active a volcano is. They draw maps that show which areas are most dangerous and what will happen in another eruption.

Predicting eruptions

Scientists take measurements to see if **magma** is moving under the volcano. They study gases from the volcano's **vent**. If they find sulphur dioxide in the gases, they know the magma is moving upwards. They check the ground for small **earthquakes** using a tool called a **seismometer**. Earthquakes are a sign that magma is moving.

In 1991 scientists predicted that Mount Pinatubo was going to erupt. They spotted hundreds of tiny earthquakes and found sulphur dioxide gas. People around the volcano moved to safety. Tens of thousands of people were saved.

GROUND MOVEMENTS

GPS stands for global positioning system. It is used by car navigation systems. Vulcanologists use GPS to find out if the ground is moving on a volcano. If the volcano bulges, it shows magma is moving and the volcano will erupt.

▲ A heat-sensing photograph of the Italian volcano Stromboli shows the temperature in different colours. The red areas are hot. They are covered in new lava.

THE TEN MOST DESTRUCTIVE VOLCANOES

When	Where	Casualties
1815	Tambora, Indonesia	92,000
1883	Krakatau, Indonesia	36,500
1902	Mont Pelée, Martinique	29,000
1985	Nevado del Ruiz, Colombia	23,000
1792	Mount Unzen, Japan	14,300
1783	Laki, Iceland	9,350
1919	Kelud, Indonesia	5,100
1882	Galunggung, Indonesia	4,000
1631	Vesuvius, Italy	3,500
79 CE	Vesuvius, Italy	3,350

FURTHER INFORMATION

Books

Earth's Changing Landscape: Earthquakes and Volcanoes by Chris Oxlade (Franklin Watts, 2004)

Horrible Geography: Violent Volcanoes by Anita Ganeri (Scholastic, 1999)

Natural Disasters: Volcanoes by Anita Ganeri (Wayland, 2007)

Our Violent Earth: Volcanoes by Fiona Waters (Wayland, 2005)

Websites

www.volcanoes.com

Contains hundreds of links to volcano sites.

www.swisseduc.ch/stromboli

Site dedicated to eruptions of Stromboli, but also photographs and videos of other volcanoes.

Videos/DVDs

Eyewitness: Volcano (Dorling Kindersley, 2000)

National Geographic: Forces of Nature directed by George Casey (1999; DVD: 2004)

Volcano: Nature's Inferno (National Geographic, 2000)

GLOSSARY

ash   Powder made of tiny pieces of rock like glass.

ash cloud   A large cloud of ash blown into the air by a volcano.

boundary   Where two tectonic plates meet.

caldera   A giant hole made when the ground collapses into an empty magma chamber.

cinder cone   A volcano made from a heap of cinders.

cinders   Small pieces of red or black rock filled with bubbles.

composite cone   A steep-sided volcano made of layers of ash and lava.

constructive boundary   A boundary where tectonic plates move apart and new rock forms in the gap.

crater   A bowl-shaped hole in the top of a volcano.

crust   The solid top layer of the Earth.

destructive boundary   A boundary where one tectonic plate dips beneath another.

earthquake   A shaking of the ground, often causing buildings to fall down and roads to break up.

forge   The place where a blacksmith works, making things from red-hot iron.

hot spot   An area in the middle of a tectonic plate where magma rises from beneath, forming a volcano.

lava   Molten or solid rock that has come from a volcano.

magma   Molten rock deep within the Earth.

magma chamber   A space beneath a volcano where magma collects.

molten   Melted into a liquid.

mud flow   A mix of ash and water making a river of mud.

pyroclastic flow   A thick cloud of red-hot ash and rock that flows down the sides of a volcano.

seismometer   A device for measuring movements of the ground.

shield volcano   A low, wide volcano made from layers of lava flow.

spreading ridge   A chain of underwater volcanoes formed when tectonic plates move apart.

tectonic plate   One of the giant pieces that make up the Earth's crust.

tuff   A type of rock made from pressed layers of volcanic ash.

vent   A hole in the middle of a volcano, through which ash and lava escape.

INDEX

Page numbers in **bold** refer to illustrations.